Renfrew

in old picture postcards volume 2

John Fyfe Anderson

European Library ZALTBOMMEL / THE NETHERLANDS

About the author:

John Fyfe Anderson was educated at the High School of Glasgow and the Universities of Warwick, Edinburgh and Strathclyde. He has a special interest in the history of the towns and villages of Renfrewshire. This is his ninth book.

The author wishes to thank the following for their permission to copy postcard and photographic material: Wilson Holland for illustrations 13, 27, 47 and 72; Norman Tait for illustrations 49 and 76. The Valentine images are from the author's collection by kind permission of St. Andrew's University Library.

By the same author:

Bishopton and Langbank in old picture postcards, volumes 1 and 2
Renfrew in old picture postcards, volume 1
Kilbarchan in old picture postcards
Greenock in old picture postcards, volumes 1 and 2
Lochwinnoch in old picture postcards
Johnstone in old picture postcards

BACK IN TIME

GB ISBN 90 288 6691 4
© 2002 European Library – Zaltbommel/The Netherlands

European Library
post office box 49
NL – 5300 AA Zaltbommel/The Netherlands
telephone: 0031 418 513144
fax: 0031 418 515515
e-mail: publisher@eurobib.nl

Introduction

Renfrew is situated on a local plain that extends from the base of the Kilpatrick Hills to the rising ground to the north of Paisley. It was originally built by David I upon the north bank of one of the branches of the Clyde and was created a Royal Burgh between 1124 and 1127. Since that time the surface along the river Clyde has undergone a considerable change. The marshy woodlands which formerly covered both banks have disappeared and the Clyde which formerly spread and flowed among numerous islands is now confined to a narrow channel. The Clyde is now half a mile from Renfrew. It is thought that the site of Renfrew was originally chosen for its strategic position on the Clyde.

Before the Romans invaded Scotland in 80 A.D. Renfrew was included in the part of Scotland known as Strathclyde, which belonged to the Brythons or Britons, a Celtic people who were Welsh speaking. Renfrew was formerly known as Rhenfrew, Ranfrew or Reinfraw. One meaning of the derivation of Renfrew is 'a point of land between the flow of the waters'. Another derivation of Renfrew is from 'Rein-froach' which means 'the heath lands'. In past times the lands which surrounded Renfrew were overgrown with heath or heather.

Walter Fitzalan (1147-1177) was created High Steward of Scotland by David I and he was given grants of land, the principal portion of these grants being in the western part of Lanarkshire, which covered an area of 245 square miles that was known as the Barony of Renfrew. Walter Fitzalan was the first Baron of Renfrew. In 1404 the title of Baron of Renfrew was conferred upon the heir to the Scottish throne. The Kingdoms of Scotland and England were united in 1707 to form a single Kingdom of Great Britain. Queen Anne was the monarch at that time. However, the tradition still continues whereby the eldest son of the British monarch assumes the title of Baron of Renfrew. H.R.H. the Prince of Wales is the twenty-ninth Baron of Renfrew.

The castle of Renfrew, long disappeared, became a royal residence. The Wars of Independence between 1296 and 1328 raised the profile of Renfrew and its castle. English forces occupied both the town and castle on various occasions. Walter Stewart, the sixth Baron of Renfrew, commanded the 'stout men of Strathgryffe' at the Battle of Bannockburn in 1314 when the Scots under Robert I defeated the English forces under Edward II. It was Robert III who confirmed Renfrew's status as a Royal Burgh in 1397.

In 1710 the historian George Crawfurd described Renfrew in the following terms:

> The town consists of one principal street about half a mile in length, with some small lanes; it has a spacious market-place and a handsome Town-house with a steeple covered with lead. […] This burgh had once some little foreign trade, but the business in which its inhabitants are mostly employed now is trade to Ireland.

In 1792 there was one bleachfield in Renfrew, a soap and candle work, a few thread mills and about one hundred and twenty people who operated looms, most of whom were employed by manufacturers in Paisley. Writing in 1811 the historian George Robertson described Renfrew as 'a clean neat enough cottage – kind of town, consisting of a single street with houses on each side, one storey high, covered with thatch'. He added that Renfrew did not seem to have increased much in size or importance since the time Crawfurd was describing it over a hundred years previously.

In 1791 the population of Renfrew was 1,013 persons. By 1841 this figure had increased to 2,027. At the beginning of the twentieth century in 1901 it had increased to 9,296 and by 1951 had reached 17,091. The present population is 20,450.

At a later period Renfrew was famous for its shipyards. The following firms were located in the town: Barr and Macnab from 1838 till circa 1850; J. Henderson, 1848-1861; Henderson and Coulbourne, 1861-1874, Lobnitz and Coulbourne, 1874-1880; Lobnitz and company, 1880-1961. Hoby was in business from 1850-1861 and Simons-Lobnitz from 1961 until circa 1970.

Tennant's chemical works in Tennant Street was established in 1844 when thirty-five people were employed there. Alan Stewart established an iron foundry in Renfrew in 1864. Clark's Bleach Works was located at the east end of the burgh. This later became Bell's Dye works. By 1959 the following firms were listed as operating in Renfrew: British Oil and Coke Mills; Silcox; Carntyne Steel Castings; Scottish Cables; Metal Containers; Clyde Rubber Works; Scottish Paints; J.O. Buchanan, Oil Refiners; Braehead Power Station.

The firm of Babcock and Wilcox Ltd. opened a factory in Renfrew in 1895. This was an American firm which was established in Clydebank in 1882. By the beginning of the twentieth century there were 1,400 people who were employed at Babcock and Wilcox. At that time there were railway connections to Glasgow and Paisley. There were also electric tramcars. A further major development was Hillington Industrial Estate, which was established in 1938 and at that time was within the burgh boundary. This was the first industrial estate of its type in Scotland.

During the First World War (1914-1918) the workers in the shipyards were employed in building ships for the Royal Navy. The firm of Babcock and Wilcox manufactured marine boilers for naval ships. A large factory was also built at Babcock's in order to produce shells for the armed forces. Women as well as men were employed in this work.

During the Second World War (1939-1945) Renfrew suffered bomb damage in several locations as a result of enemy raids. At the time of the Clydebank Blitz on 13th March 1941 the wharf near the Renfrew Ferry was destroyed due to bombing. New organizations were established as a result of the outbreak of the Second World War. These included the Home Guard, Royal Observer Corps and Air Raid Precautions, later known as the Civil Defence Corps. Many local people made a considerable contribution to life in Renfrew as a result of their involvement with the above organizations.

Renfrew has gone through many changes in its long history. A major change occurred during the second half of the nineteenth century when the commercial and industrial life of the town developed. As a result Renfrew became a busy and prosperous place. In 1997 the town celebrated the sixth hundredth anniversary of the charter confirming its status as a Royal Burgh. As a result of local government organization in 1975 Renfrew has lost its burgh status. It is now administered by Renfrewshire Council, which is based in Paisley. However, Renfrew still retains its special character with distinctive landmarks such as the Town Hall and the spire of the Old Parish Church. A recent development has been the building of the Braehead Shopping Centre, which is historically part of the Royal Burgh of Renfrew. A large number of retail outlets are situated there and attract thousands of customers from all areas in the west of Scotland. In 2001 it became possible to sail from Glasgow to Braehead with the introduction of a regular service on the 'Pride of the Clyde' echoing the famous 'Clutha' steamers of a previous era.

The writer of the entry for Renfrew in the Third Statistical Account stated the following:

> Renfrew as a community is compact, highly industrialised and progressive. With a population made up of so many different elements, and with the large centres of Paisley and Glasgow so near at hand, the task of creating a full yet independent community life and spirit is very great; nevertheless it is in great measure achieved.

It is true that there is less industry in Renfrew as a result of the decline of shipbuilding. However, the community spirit does remain.

This book contains a wide variety of illustrations which show different aspects of life in Renfrew during the late nineteenth century and the earlier decades of the twentieth century. The people of Renfrew have made a considerable contribution to the life of the nation in times of peace and war. Indeed Renfrew occupies a notable position in the history of the realm.

Bibliography

M. Burgess, *World War 2 in Renfrewshire*, Renfrew District Council, 1995

J.A. Dunn, *History of Renfrew*, Town Council of Renfrew, n.d.

F.H. Groome (Ed.), *Ordnance Gazetteer of Scotland*, vol. 6, Edinburgh, 1885

Rev. D.M. Swanson, *The Parish and Burgh of Renfrew*, Third Statistical Account of Scotland, vol. Xl, Glasgow 1962

F.A. Walker, *The South Clyde Estuary*, Edinburgh, 1986

Workers' Educational Association Renfrew Reminiscence Group, *Renfrew Remembered*, n.d.

Files of the Paisley and Renfrewshire Gazette

Renfrew Directories

1. Local views

This postcard displays four views of Renfrew in former days. Trams are in evidence in the views of the Pudzeoch and Ferry Road and also in Hairst Street. A sailing ship is seen moored in the Pudzeoch. Two young girls with their distinctive hats are seen standing on the Ferry Green by the River Clyde. The great mansion of Blythswood in its magnificent grounds is also seen here. This postcard also includes the coat of arms of Renfrew. The Lord Lyon King of Arms granted them on 7th July 1676. The motto in Latin 'Deus Gubernat Navem' means 'God is the pilot of the ship'. This emphasises Renfrew's connection with the River Clyde and ships. The coat of arms includes the Lion Rampant, which is the Royal Standard of Scotland, and also the arms of the Stewarts. Renfrew's coat of arms can be seen carved above the front door of the Town Hall and also at the police station in Inchinnan Road.

INCHINNAN ROAD AND WAR MEMORIAL, RENFREW.   A 3829

2. Inchinnan Road and War Memorial

An interesting selection of vehicles is seen in this view, but traffic is very light compared to the present day. The War Memorial is visible in the right foreground. The dome of the Victory Baths can also be seen on the right of this view. The Victory Baths were built in 1921 and designed by T.G. Abercrombie. This building was presented to Renfrew by Sir Frederick and Lady Lobnitz. The firm of Lobnitz and Company was established in 1895. It specialized in the production of dredgers, sand pumps, rock breakers and hopper barges. In 1960 the firm amalgamated with William Simons and Company and became known as Simons-Lobnitz and Company. The two advertisement hoardings on the gable-end in the foreground have been displayed by the Scottish Co-operative Wholesale Society.

WAR MEMORIAL, RENFREW.

3. War Memorial

The following words have been inscribed on the side of the war memorial: 'In memory of the men of Renfrew who sacrificed their lives for their country in the Great War 1914-1918. Their name liveth for ever.' The names of the various regiments in which these men served are also inscribed on the memorial. These include the Argyll and Sutherland Highlanders, the Highland Light Infantry, the Cameron Highlanders and the Royal Scots Fusiliers. The letters 'R.N.' are inscribed beside the names of the men who served in the Royal Navy. There are now two tablets of stone at the base of the war memorial on which are inscribed the names of the men of Renfrew who lost their lives in the Second World War.

The Jail, Renfrew

4. Police Station

On the right of this view is Renfrew Police Station. This building was formally opened on 13th March 1910 in the presence of all the Renfrew town councillors and burgh officials. Others who attended the ceremony included the chief constables of Govan, Partick, Johnstone and Greenock. Provost McKechnie of Govan was also in attendance. The proceedings at the opening ceremony were commenced by the architect, Mr. A.R. Paterson, who asked Provost Robert Anderson to accept a golden key in the name of the contractors. The Provost then declared the new building open and invited the assembled company to enter. An inspection of the building then took place. All of those present expressed their admiration of the design of this new building, which cost £60,000. Afterwards light refreshments were served in the gymnasium. The new police station was built because of the rapidly increasing population of the burgh and also as a consequence of Government requirements. In 1910 the chief constable of Renfrew was Captain William Robb, who had been appointed to the position in the previous year. He served as chief constable until 1930.

5. Ferry Road, Renfrew

An open-topped tram and a horse-drawn cart are the only traffic to be seen in this view of Ferry Road. On the right is the Renfrew Canal, which was known locally as the 'Pudzeoch'. The canal was built in the last quarter of the eighteenth century as a result of an agreement between the Burgh of Renfrew and the Laird of Elderslie. The construction of the canal was intended to restore Renfrew's status as a leading port on the Clyde. The 'Pudzeoch' ran from the Clyde to Canal Street. It was infilled in the early years of the twentieth century.

HIGH STREET, RENFREW. A.3828. (JV)

6. High Street

This view shows High Street when the trams still operated. This is a somewhat deserted scene with few pedestrians and little traffic. All of the buildings on the right of High Street have been removed, with the exception of the bank building at Renfrew Cross. A variety of new retail outlets and other premises have been built on the right of High Street. There are now attractive flower beds in the area near the Town Hall, where the tramlines are in this view. The dominating position of the Town Hall is evident here.

HIGH STREET, RENFREW

A 3849

7. High Street

The breadth of High Street is in evidence here as the single-decker bus proceeds towards Renfrew Cross. A tramcar at the Cross is dwarfed by the Town Hall. The spire of Renfrew Old Parish Church is on the left of this view. The Ross Tomb is located in the Old Parish Church. It is contained within an arched recess on which the following is inscribed: 'Here lies Sir John Ross, Knight late Baron of Hawkhead and Marjory his wife. Pray for those who died.' When the vault was opened in 1908 the earliest dated coffin found was that of James, sixth Lord Ross, who died in 1633. It is not clear which Sir John Ross is commemorated in the tomb. The first Sir John Ross is mentioned in 1367. In the late fifteenth century King James IV created a descendant, also named Sir John Ross, the first Lord Ross of Hawkhead. The last member of the family to hold the title was George, thirteenth Lord Ross, who died in 1754.

8. Paisley Road from St. Andrew's Cross

This postcard has a misprint because 'Risley Road' has been written instead of 'Paisley Road'. Tramlines are seen here at St. Andrew's Cross. The block of tenements to the left have been demolished while those on the right remain in position. The lamp-posts which can be faintly discerned on the left have been removed.

9. St. Andrew's Cross

A group of children and adults are seen here standing on the site which was later to be occupied by the War Memorial. An open-topped tram is visible on the left of this view while on the right there is a horse-drawn cart. There is another horse-drawn conveyance beside the lamp-post in the centre of the picture. The shops on Inchinnan Road beneath the tenemental properties include a draper, watchmaker, tea-room and baker. Renfrew Post Office can be seen on the far right of this view.

10. Coronation Tram

Trams formerly operated from Glasgow to Renfrew. This service of electric trams began in 1902 and was extended to Porterfield Road in 1932. The tram service ceased to operate in 1957. The rails on the route to Porterfield Road were removed in 1962 and those on Paisley Road in 1963. This photograph was taken on 17th April 1954 at Renfrew Ferry. It shows Coronation tram number 1268. This tram was one of a fleet operated by Glasgow Corporation Transport. The coat of arms of the City of Glasgow can be seen above the driver's window.

24422   SHIPBUILDING AT RENFREW   VALENTINES SERIES

11. Shipbuilding at Renfrew

The first shipbuilding firm in Renfrew was Barr and Macnab, which was established in 1844. This firm was later acquired by James Henderson and Son who began business in 1847. Henderson's first ship was a paddle steamer of 140 tons which was built for the Anchor Line. This firm began to build dredgers and in 1880 was reorganized under the name Lobnitz and Company. William Simons and company began business in Greenock in 1810, then moved to Canada in 1812. However, the firm was re-established at Greenock in 1818 and remained there until 1850 when it moved to Whiteinch. In 1861 William Simons and company relocated to Renfrew and remained there for the next hundred years. This firm was among the first to develop a tool that was capable of deepening and smoothing the river bed and removing the debris. Andrew Brown was responsible for designing this item. He had originally been employed as the engineering manager at A. and J. Inglis and Company. His considerable abilities were recognized by William Simons and company and when the firm moved to Renfrew in 1861 he was appointed as a director.

BABCOCK & WILCOX L^{TD} MARINE WORKS, MOORPARK, RENFREW.

12. Babcock and Wilcox Ltd.

On 11th June 1930 the Prince of Wales (later King Edward VIII and the Duke of Windsor) visited the works of Babcock and Wilcox Ltd. As his car approached the main streets of Renfrew on that day he was cheered by large crowds who lined the route along Porterfield Road. Tenements in the area and other buildings were decorated with Union Jacks and the local children also displayed flags. The Prince of Wales was greeted with cheers by workers and office girls at the entrance to Babcock and Wilcox in French Street. The Prince was also loudly cheered when he left the works and the police had difficulty in restraining the crowd from approaching too close to his car. Babcock and Wilcox Ltd., specialists in marine engineering, was established in Renfrew in 1895. The firm was not greatly affected by the trade depressions of the 1920s and 1930s and thus was able to expand. At a later period Babcock and Wilcox began to produce nuclear plant and equipment.

Babcock & Wilcox Ltd, Renfrew.

13. Babcock and Wilcox Ltd.

The firm of Babcock and Wilcox was originally located in Clydebank. A new factory was later built in Renfrew on a 160 acre site at the top of Porterfield Road and about a thousand workers came to work there from Clydebank in 1887. The firm gained a worldwide reputation for their manufacture of boiler installations and many other types of engineering products. Babcock and Wilcox's research centre in High Street was erected in 1947. By 1971 the firm employed six thousand people of whom almost a third lived in Renfrew. The firm is now known as Mitsui Babcock Energy Ltd. at its premises in High Street. The factory in Porterfield Road is known as Mitsui Babcock Energy Services Ltd.

Shipyard Gates, Renfrew.

14. Shipyard gates

At the end of this street are the entrance gates to the works of Lobnitz and Company. This firm dates from 1895 and specialized in the production of dredgers and suction pumps, rock breakers and hopper barges. During the Second World War Lobnitz and Company designed and built the 'Mulberry Harbours' which were described by Prime Minister Winston Churchill as 'piers for use on the beaches'. The finished product weighed about one thousand tons. They were used on the Normandy beaches for the D-Day landings in June 1944. Lobnitz and Company amalgamated with William Simons and company in 1959 and assumed the name of Simons-Lobnitz and Company. At its peak the new company employed about 2,000 men. In 1960 the two firms became part of G. and J. Weir and Company of Cathcart. The business was transferred to A. and J. Stephens at Linthouse in 1964 and by 1969 no trace of any industrial plant remained.

Canal Street, Renfrew

15. Canal Street

Two men on the left face the camera in this scene. On the right a woman stands beside the premises of Mrs. Colin P. Baird, draper, which were located at the Bank buildings, Renfrew Cross. The former railway track can be faintly discerned above the embankment in the distance. There is a notable absence of traffic in Canal Street.

INCHINNAN ROAD FROM ROBERTSON PARK, RENFREW.

A.3852.

16. Inchinnan Road

A solitary cyclist has stopped in a deserted Inchinnan Road in this scene on a sunny day many years ago. The crow-stepped gable of the police station is clearly visible here. Next to it are the Victory Baths which continue to be a well-used facility for the people of Renfrew. The war memorial can be faintly discerned at St. Andrew's Cross.

INCHINNAN ROAD, RENFREW.

17. Inchinnan Road

This tranquil scene emphasises the rural aspect of Inchinnan Road in the early decades of the twentieth century. The boundary wall on the right is that of the Blythswood Estate which is now occupied by a variety of retail outlets. This road leads on to the village of Inchinnan.

Ferry from Yoker side, Renfrew.

777/44

18. Ferry from Yoker side

The houses on the south bank of the Clyde are in Renfrew. An early open-topped motor car is seen driving onto the second steam ferry. There are still two ferries for pedestrians between Renfrew and Yoker. These ferries transport almost 200,000 passengers across the Clyde every year.

19. Renfrew ferry.
This is the second steam ferry which operated at Renfrew. An early open-topped car with brass headlights can be seen on the right of this view from the first decade of the twentieth century. Two cyclists are also waiting near the ferry. A group of people of all ages are seen here and they exhibit the various fashions which were prevalent at the time.

20. Yoker and Renfrew ferry
This was the second steam ferry which was in operation at Renfrew from 1897 until 1912. The first steam-driven ferry began service at Renfrew in 1868. It had only one chain which was in position at the west side of the ferry. That ferry also had hand-operated landing platforms which resulted in difficulties when making a landing at low tides.

RENFREW FERRY. A 3821.

21. Renfrew ferry

Two cars and a group of foot passengers are seen arriving on the south bank of the Clyde at Renfrew having taken the ferry from Yoker. This ferry was built in 1935 by Fleming and Ferguson of Paisley. It was operated by the Clyde Navigation Trust. The ferry had a steel double chain and was 68 ft long with a breadth of 48 ft.

RENFREW FERRY.

THIS NEW FERRY WHICH CAN TAKE ABOUT TWENTY AVERAGE SIZE MOTOR CARS. HAS SPEEDED UP TRAFFIC
CROSSING THE CLYDE AT THIS POINT.

22. Renfrew ferry

A group of people wait at Renfrew for the ferry as it crosses the Clyde from Yoker. This ferry could accommodate twenty cars in the 1930s. In this view it is dwarfed by the massive pylon of the Clyde Valley Electric Power Company. Following the launching ceremony of the 'Empress of Britain' on 11th June 1930, the Prince of Wales returned to Renfrew by the ferry and drove through the town en route to Eastwood Park. On this occasion many people lined Ferry Road and Canal Street. A contemporary newspaper report made reference to the excitement of the waiting crowd and also stated what 'the Royal visitor again received a demonstration of patriotic fervour'.

Renfrew Ferry.

23. Renfrew ferry

The Renfrew ferry has just arrived from Yoker in this scene. The man on the right who has just disembarked from the ferry appears to be in a considerable hurry in contrast to the two women who are walking slowly towards it. The cars are waiting to drive off the ferry while a solitary cyclist precedes them. Some foot passengers can be seen standing on the deck on the right of the ferry.

Paisley Road, Moorpark, Renfrew.

24. Paisley Road

The tramlines can still be seen in this view of Paisley Road in the early decades of the twentieth century. The long row of tenements on the left dominate this scene. The church on the right is no longer used for religious purposes. It is now known as Koko's and is open on every day of the week for birthday parties and adventure play. There is also a nursery for children.

PAISLEY ROAD, RENFREW

25. Paisley Road

The substantial tenements of Paisley Road are shown to advantage in this view on a sunny day in the 1920s. A varied group on the left pose for the photographer. In the immediate foreground are the premises of J. Orr, tobacconist and confectioner. Part of Porterfield Road can be seen on the left of this view.

26. Paisley Road

A group of young children stand in Paisley Road in the early decades of the twentieth century. The public house on the left has been extended and is now known as the 'Dog and Sausage'. New housing has been built between the tenements in the foreground. The Olympic Car Centre is also located in this area.

Paisley Rd and Donaldson Drive, Renfrew.

27. Paisley Road and Donaldson Drive

This shows Paisley Road before the tramlines were laid. Judging by the stones in the foreground it would appear that repair work is taking place at this location. The two men who are standing by the handcart pose for the photographer.

28. Paisley Road

A solitary woman walks in Paisley Road in the early years of the twentieth century. A tram is also visible and is proceeding towards Renfrew. Good quality housing is in evidence on both sides of the road. In the distance the tenements in Porterfield Road can be faintly discerned.

BLYTHSWOOD HOUSE RENFREW.

29. Blythswood House

Royal visitors often resided at Blythswood House. In September 1927 the Duke and Duchess of York were in residence there. The Duke of York later became King George VI in 1936 as a result of the abdication of his elder brother, King Edward VIII. The Duchess of York assumed the title of Queen Elizabeth and later became well-known as the Queen Mother. On Wednesday, 21st September 1927 the Duchess of York planted a tree in the grounds of Blythswood House. A contemporary newspaper report stated that the weather was very unfavourable, but the Duchess continued with the ceremony despite these conditions. The Duke of York had planted a tree in the grounds on a previous visit. In 1876 King Edward VII and Queen Alexandra, who were then Prince and Princess of Wales, resided at Blythswood when they came to lay the foundation stone of the General Post Office in George Square, Glasgow. In 1907 the future King George V and Queen Mary also resided at this great mansion-house on the occasion of their laying foundation stones at Glasgow Royal Infirmary and Rothesay Dock.

Blythswood House, Renfrew

30. Blythswood House

Blythswood House was built in 1820-1822 and had a total of 118 rooms. It was situated within extensive grounds, where there were two curling ponds, a farm, a coal-mine, a cricket pitch, two tennis courts, two bowling greens, and a nine-hole and nineteen-hole golf course. There was a large staff of estate workers. A group of gardeners tended apricot, fig, melon and plum trees in the kitchen garden. Roses and camellias grew in the flower garden. The grounds also contained a magnificent collection of trees, some of great age. The demolition of Blythswood House in 1935 was a great loss to Renfrew. During the demolition an underground passage was discovered just below the strong-room. It is thought that this may have led at one time to the old Renfrew Castle.

Blythswood House, Renfrew

31. Blythswood House

This is a magnificent view of Blythswood House showing its rear entrance. The high quality of the formal garden is in evidence here. The estate of Blythswood was formerly known as Ranfield. It was purchased in 1654 by Colin Campbell who became Provost of Glasgow in 1648. He also purchased the lands of Blythswood in Glasgow. This resulted in the change of name of the estate at Renfrew to Blythswood. The Campbell family originally possessed a mansion in the Saltmarket in Glasgow and also a similar property in the Bridgegate.

Blythswood House, Renfrew.

I think your mother will know this house very well. J. L. M.

32. Blythswood House

One of the most notable visitors to this great mansion was Queen Victoria, who arrived here on 22nd August 1888. The reason for Queen Victoria's presence at Blythswood House was to visit Glasgow in order to open the new City Chambers in George Square and also to attend the first International Exhibition which was being held in that year. Grandstands and ornamental arches were erected at Inchinnan Road and in Hairst Street for Queen Victoria's visit. Grandstands were also erected on both sides of Fulbar Street and outside the Town Hall. After arrival at Fulbar Street Station the Queen proceeded to Blythswood House, the residence of Sir Archibald and Lady Campbell. Her Majesty later returned from Blythswood House in an open carriage which was drawn by four horses with a mounted escort. The carriage halted at the balcony opposite the Town Hall, where the magistrates, town councillors and officials were assembled. Provost Daniel Wright gave an address of welcome and presented Queen Victoria with a silver gilt casket. The Queen handed a written reply to Provost Wright which read as follows: *Your loyal and dutiful address gives me great satisfaction. It affords me much pleasure to have this opportunity of visiting a Royal Burgh so closely connected with the ancient history of my Kingdom of Scotland and of seeing a district which has done so much in modern times for the prosperity of my United Kingdom.*

Elderslie House, Renfrew.

33. Elderslie House

Elderslie House was situated near the left-hand bank of the River Clyde not far from Renfrew and about 40 yards from where the old Inch Castle stood. The building of this mansion house commenced in 1777. It was a four-storeyed building with a pavilion roof and its dimensions were 90 feet long and 60 feet broad. Elderslie House was located in the middle of a pleasant green park. The builder of this property was Alexander Speirs. Alexander Speirs was born on 14th September 1714. He was a partner in the banking firm of Speirs, Murdoch and company and was one of the founders of the Glasgow Arms Bank. He also possessed over ten thousand acres in Renfrewshire. However, Alexander Speirs only resided in Elderslie House for a few months as he died in December 1782, the building of the property having only been completed in the autumn of the same year. Alexander Speirs married Mary Buchanan, who was the daughter of Archibald Buchanan of Auchentorlie. They had a family of four sons and six daughters. The Speirs family resided in Elderslie House until the death of Captain Archibald Alexander Speirs, who was the great-grandson of Alexander Speirs. Elderslie House was demolished in 1924. Braehead Power Station and various factories were later erected on the site of Elderslie House and its grounds.

ROBERTSON PARK, RENFREW   No. 3

34. Robertson Park

This park was formally opened on 19th October 1912. It was the gift of Mr. William Robertson, who was a native of Renfrew and also the owner of the Glen Line of steamships. There was a large turnout of people at the opening ceremony, with flags and bunting being displayed at the main entrance to the park in Inchinnan Road. The members of Renfrew Town Council and invited guests assembled in front of the police station. The company then entered the park and halted at the flagstaff where the donor, Mr. John Robertson, unfurled the flag. The main part of the ceremony took place at the bandstand. Afterwards the company assembled in the bandstand and congratulatory speeches were made. Among those present were the Rev. Lord Blythswood, Sir William Bilsland, Sir Thomas Mason, Mr. A.A. Hagart Speirs and Provost Muir MacKean of Paisley. Provost Robert Anderson stated the following at the opening ceremony: *Our ancient and royal burgh of Renfrew, has during its long life, seen many varied and historic events; but the opening today of this beautiful park takes rank amongst the foremost of them. In olden times the Stewart Kings resided in our midst at the Castlehill, and in modern times Kings too resided in our midst at the Manor of Blythswood. Today we are seeing the consummation of a gift by a King of industry, Mr. William Robertson, a son of the burgh and one of our honorary burgesses.*

Robertson Park Gates, Inchinnan Road, Renfrew.

35. Inchinnan Road

The entrance gates to the Robertson Park can be seen on the right of this view of the early twentieth century. The tenements which can be seen in Hairst Street have been demolished. The War Memorial at St. Andrew's Cross had not been erected when this scene was photographed. The lamp-post shown here has been removed.

ROBERTSON PARK, RENFREW.   No. 2

36. Robertson Park

A young boy stands outside the entrance to the Robertson Park in Paisley Road. It appears to have rained recently judging by the muddy surface of the road. The bandstand in the park can be seen in the distance.

Porterfield Road, Renfrew.

37. Porterfield Road

This is a scene from the early 1900s. Only pedestrians can be seen in this view. There is no traffic whatsoever. The writer of this postcard marked his own place of residence with a cross and this is visible on the left of the picture. At the beginning of last century no building had taken place on the land to the left of this view. A hedge can also be seen. The factory buildings in the distance are those of Babcock and Wilcox Ltd.

MANSE STREET, RENFREW
24424
VALENTINES SERIES

38. Manse Street

This view shows Manse Street on a sunny day at the beginning of the twentieth century. All of the houses shown here have been demolished. They were situated near Renfrew Cross and from a twenty-first-century perspective appear to have added considerable character to the town in former days. The second building on the left with the crow-stepped gable was where Robert Lang was in business as a spirit merchant. The front of the property on the immediate left was on Canal Street. It can be seen that Manse Street was laid with cobblestones.

39. Broad Loan

This view shows a quiet scene in Broad Loan at the beginning of the twentieth century. A group of children pose for the camera while standing in the street with no worries about oncoming traffic. A horse and cart is the only mode of transport to be seen. The three men on the right are captured by the camera for posterity.

SANDY ROAD, RENFREW

40. Sandy Road

A group of boys – one with a bicycle – stand on the pavement in this scene on an otherwise deserted Sandy Road. On the left telegraph poles and a solitary lamp-post can be seen. There are now many parked cars to be seen on this road. In 1936 Sandy Road was the first location in Renfrew where electricity was used for street lighting.

Fauldshead Road Renfrew.

41. Fauldshead Road

The spire of Renfrew Old Parish Church can be seen in the distance. Council house properties can be seen on the right of this view with the differing styles of private housing on the left side of the road. A total of 1,254 council houses were built in Renfrew between 1919 and 1939 and 1,009 in the period 1945-1959. The first council houses in Renfrew were erected in Victory Gardens in 1919 shortly after the conclusion of hostilities in the First World War.

INCHINNAN AND RENFREW SWING BRIDGE

42. Inchinnan and Renfrew swing bridge

The original bridge at this location was built over a canal which was constructed by the Corporation of Paisley because there was not sufficient depth for vessels in the White Cart due to the presence of rocks. It was in 1787 when a wooden swing bridge was built here. The cost of the bridge was estimated to be £1,900 and the construction of the canal cost about £4,000. Many steamers formerly used the canal. As a result of the increase in the number of vessels using the canal a new bridge was required. The wooden swing bridge was demolished in 1919. A temporary bridge was then erected before the present steel bascule bridge was opened in 1923. Strengthening work has recently taken place on this bridge.

43. Renfrew Town Hall

On 30th October 1879 a grand ball was held at the Town Hall to celebrate the formal opening of the reconstructed building following a fire in the previous year. The proceedings began at 9 p.m. with Provost Allan Stewart leading his partner in the quadrille. Mr. Adam's quadrille band from Glasgow was present on that evening. A contemporary newspaper report stated: 'Dancing was kept up with vigour by the company for several hours.' During the evening Mr. John Forrester provided supper for the guests in the lower apartments of the building. An extensive menu was offered on this occasion. There were rounds of beef, galantines of veal, boned turkeys and roast chickens. There were also Cumberland hams, ox tongues and French game pies. In addition there were larded pheasants, partridges and lobster salads. There was an enormous selection for dessert with a meringue of peaches, compote of apples, chocolate tarts, Berlin tarts, French pastry, Madeira jellies, Macedonia jellies and Italian cream. There was also a buffet providing tea, coffee, ices, fruit, cakes, Moselle and claret cups. The committee which organized the ball consisted of Dr. J.R.M. Robertson, Mr. A.M. Herron, Town Clerk; Mr. McGlashan, Rector of Blythswood Testimonial School; and Mr. Cameron, Town Chamberlain. It is recorded that the assembled company at this grand ball finally departed shortly after 3 a.m. on Friday, 31st October 1879.

TOWN HALL, RENFREW.

44. Town Hall

On his visit to Renfrew on 11th June 1930 the Prince of Wales halted at the Town Hall on his way to Clydebank to perform the launching ceremony of the 'Empress of Britain' from the yard of John Brown and Co. He was welcomed by Provost John McGregor, Town Clerk Mr. E.D. Anderson, and a number of Town Councillors, including the magistrates who were wearing their robes. The Prince signed the visitors' book which lay open on a table in front of the building. Provost McGregor in greeting the royal visitor stated the following: *Your Royal Highness, as Prince of Wales and Baron Renfrew, we again welcome you to this royal burgh. We greatly appreciate your kindness in breaking your journey here, and we ask you to record the event in our book of distinguished visitors which you signed before in the years 1918 and 1921.*

45. Town Hall

This is a close-up of the Town Hall from High Street. The memorial stone of the Town Hall was laid on 13th April 1872. On that day there was a great procession in Renfrew. It proceeded along the following route: Meadowside Street, Ferry Road, Canal Street, Croft Street, Mill Vennel (now Millburn Way) and back along High Street to the front of the Town Hall. The Grand Marshal of the procession was James Dobbie, Superintendent of Police. The following trades took part in the procession: carters with horses, joiners, painters, engineers, plumbers, masons, patternmakers, boilermakers, blacksmiths and carpenters. Friendly Societies were also part of the procession. The Good Templars, Foresters, Shepherds, Oddfellows and Gardeners participated on this occasion. There were also the Knights of Malta, Renfrew Volunteer Corps, the Provost, magistrates and members of Renfrew Town Council, burgh officials of Renfrew and the Provost and magistrates of Paisley. The Town Council met in their new building on 18th September 1873 and decided that they would celebrate the opening of the Town Hall on 17th October with a festival to which the elite of the county of Renfrewshire would be invited. This would include the newly elected Member of Parliament, Colonel Archibald Campbell of Blythswood. The Town Council also made the necessary arrangements for a ball which would take place in the Town Hall a week later.

Town Hall Renfrew

Ferry Road and Picture Palace, Renfrew

JV 74618

46. Ferry Road and Picture Palace
This building was formerly the Renfrew Regal Cinema. It is now the Regal Bingo Hall. The bridge on the left at one time carried railway traffic but no longer exists. The railway track can be seen on the right of this view. The power lines for the trams have been removed as has the telegraph pole.

47. Moorpark Cinema

This shows the entrance to the Moorpark Cinema in Paisley Road. The cinema was known locally as the 'Moor-kie'. The cinema was entered by a close which led to the expensive seats. There was a back entrance in Porterfield Road for the cheaper seats. It cost tuppence in old money (less than 1p) for the matinee performance at the cinema. Evidently, local boys would try and gain admission by climbing up the corrugated roof. However, the usherette on duty would hear the sound on the roof and order the boys to come down. In this view the films being shown are 'Shoulder Arms' starring Charlie Chaplin and 'Canyon Passage' with Dana Andrews, Susan Hayward, Brian Donlevy, Patricia Roc and Hoagy Carmichael.

TRINITY U.F. CHURCH, RENFREW.

48. Trinity Church

Trinity Church in Paisley Road was originally built for a congregation of the United Presbyterian Church. The first minister of this church was the Rev. John Hutcheson, who served from 1865 until 1877. During the ministry of the Rev. John Hogarth in 1891 the decision was made to build church halls which would seat four hundred people. A hall was also erected at Moorpark which served as a mission Sunday School. In 1900 the United Presbyterian Church united with the Free Church of Scotland and became the United Free Church. 593 United Presbyterian congregations united with 1,068 from the Free Church. In that year Trinity Church became a United Free Church congregation. A further union of the churches took place in 1929 when the United Free Church united with the Church of Scotland. As a result Trinity Church became a Church of Scotland congregation. One of the most notable ministers of Trinity Church was the Rev. Professor William Barclay, C.B.E., D.D. who was minister from 1933 until 1947. He achieved a worldwide reputation for his theological writings, particularly his Daily Study Bible, which sold millions of copies. William Barclay was Professor of Divinity and Biblical Criticism at the University of Glasgow from 1963 until 1974.

49. Renfrew Old Parish Church (1726-1860)

This church was built in 1726 and was in use until 1860. However, the walls were more than six hundred years old as they formed part of the previous church which was demolished in 1726. The church in this view was built to resemble a Greek cross with a nave and transept. It had seating for 750 people. In 1820 at a political meeting, which was held in the church, arguments took place between opposing parties and fighting occurred. There was considerable damage to walls, windows and pews. The two opposing candidates offered to pay fifty per cent of the cost of damage. The damage was so extensive that both church and school services had to be held in the town house for a considerable period. The cost of repairs was £815, which was a large sum at that time. In past centuries precentors were employed in the Church of Scotland to lead the congregation in the singing of Psalms. The following excerpt is taken from the minutes of the old parish church records of 9th January 1840: 'Owing to the backward state of the church music it was agreed to procure a well qualified precentor on the understanding that money had been given for this purpose.' A Mr. Hannah was appointed to this position. He commenced his duties on 18th May 1840. The last service in this church was held on 2nd September 1860 and there were very large attendances on that day. The preacher was the Rev. Robert Stephen, who was the parish minister from 1858 until his death in 1897.

THE PARISH CHURCH, RENFREW.   A.3853.

50. Renfrew Old Parish Church

The foundation stone of Renfrew Old Parish Church was laid on 24th May 1861. The following people were present at the ceremony: the Provost of Renfrew, William Bell, the magistrates of the Burgh, the architect of the church J.T. Rochead and the Rev. Robert Stephen, minister of the Parish. Other important gentlemen of the district were also present. On this occasion there was a procession of the Paisley, St. Mirren's and County Kilwinning Lodges of Free Masons which was preceded by the Renfrewshire Militia Band. Prayers were offered by the Rev. Robert Stephen and then Mr. James Smith of Jordanhill deposited a crystal vase containing several contemporary newspapers, a number of documents and the current coins of the realm into the cavity in the stone. A parchment scroll was also deposited and this stated the following: *This foundation stone of the Church and Parish of Renfrew was laid by William Bell, Esq., Merchant in Renfrew, Provost of the Burgh and this crystal vase was deposited by James Smith, Esq. of Jordanhill after a prayer by the Rev. Robert Stephen, minister of the Parish of Renfrew, all at Renfrew, between the hours of two and four o'clock afternoon, upon the 24th of May 1861.* This scroll also included the names of the heritors (landowners), the Town Council, contractors and other officers who were associated with the Burgh of Renfrew.

Parish Church, Renfrew

51. Renfrew Old Parish Church

This church was opened for public worship on Sunday 20th July 1862. The preacher at the morning service was the Rev. Robert Stephen, minister of the Parish. Fourteen children were baptized at that service. There was a service in the afternoon and the preacher was the Rev. Dr. Gillan of Inchinnan. There was also an evening service when the preacher was the Rev. Dr. Norman MacLeod of the Barony Church, Glasgow. There were large attendances at all of these services. Sittings in the church were previously let on an annual basis. Sittings in the previous parish church, which were the property of the burgh, cost 5p per annum. In 1889 this system changed and the kirk session were instructed by the Town Chamberlain to let the sittings at 15p each for the area and 10p for the gallery. The other sittings were held by the heritors, but these were later handed over to the kirk session. Seat rents were finally abolished in Renfrew Old Parish Church in 1957. A chancel was added in 1909 and a pipe organ was installed in 1910. There is also a stained-glass window in the chancel, which was gifted by the shipowner William Robertson in memory of Dr. Peter McLaren, who was headmaster of Blythswood Testimonial School from 1843 until 1876. There are also three smaller stained-glass windows in the chancel, which were gifted by Mr. Thomas Hill in memory of his brother, who was killed at Gallipoli in 1916.

52. Pudzeoch and Ferry Road

An open-topped tram and a sailing ship are visible in this early twentieth-century scene. The terminus for trams used to be located at Renfrew Ferry. One of the longest tram journeys was from Renfrew Ferry to Hillfoot via Paisley, Barrhead, Thornliebank and Glasgow. The fare was less than 1p. A wharf was built at Renfrew in 1837. There was also a railway line at the wharf. It also opened in 1837. Both passengers and cargoes were conveyed on the railway. Many paddle-steamers used to call at the Renfrew wharf. These included the 'Lord of the Isles', ' Madge Wildfire', 'Meg Merrilees', 'Windsor Castle', 'Benmore', 'Sultana' and the 'Victoria', which was the first Sunday steamer. However, all vessels ceased to call in 1941.

53. Bell Street

This is a view of Bell Street towards the end of the nineteenth century. The trees on the right have been removed and there are now tenements on this site. There is a noticeable lack of any kind of traffic in this view. The group of boys, who are standing on the pavement on the left, are looking at the camera. However, the group of girls on the opposite side of the street are ignoring it! The houses on the right of Bell Street remain in position, as does the tenemental block on the immediate left in this view. The block of tenements to the right of the lamp-post has been demolished and more modern properties have been erected on that site.

54. Bell Street

Some children pose for the photographer in Bell Street in the early years of the twentieth century. There is a contrast in architectural styles with the tenemental properties in the foreground and the row of terraced houses which were built in the 1860s. There is a noticeable lack of traffic in the street, thus providing a safe environment for the local children.

55. Bowling

A group of well-dressed men are involved in a game of bowls on this well-kept green. This is a scene from the late nineteenth century. Renfrew Bowling Club was established in 1851 and a committee was appointed to prepare a set of rules and regulations. A general meeting of the club was held on 12th April 1852 under the chairmanship of Provost George Boyd. At that meeting the rules and regulations were submitted and approved. Provost Boyd was the first president of Renfrew Bowling Club.

56. Fulbar Street

A group of children and some adults are seen standing in Fulbar Street towards the end of the nineteenth century. Two very young children are also visible beside the premises of D. Hillcoat, Wright and Builder. This scene behind the Town Hall has changed as a result of the erection of new buildings. The breadth of this street is notable as is the total absence of traffic. Today, large numbers of cars can be seen parked on both sides of the street.

57. High Street

This is how High Street looked in the latter decades of the nineteenth century. No traffic whatsoever is seen here. The impressive spire of Renfrew Parish Church is visible on the left of this scene. The one-storeyed properties in the immediate foreground have been demolished.

58. Hairst Street

A young boy stands in the wide expanse of an almost deserted Hairst Street in this late nineteenth century view. The distinctive tower of Renfrew Town Hall dominates the scene here. All of the two-storeyed houses on the immediate right have been demolished. The same fate occurred to the cluster of properties at the far end of the street with the exception of the Wheatsheaf Inn which was built about 1830 and is situated near the Town Hall. When this photograph was taken Renfrew Post Office was in Hairst Street and can be seen between the two lamp-posts on the left of this view.

59. Paisley Road

The somewhat muddy surface of Paisley Road is seen in this view which dates from the late nineteenth century. The tower of Trinity Church can be seen on the right of Paisley Road. The site for this church was gifted by Mr. Matthew Robin who owned 'Croft-en-Righ', which formerly stood at the corner of Queen Street and Glebe Street. The foundation of Trinity Church was laid by Sir Peter Coats in August 1864. The building of the church was completed by June 1865. Tenements have been built where the hedge is in this view. The Town Hall can just be discerned in the distance.

Moorpark School, Renfrew.

60. Moorpark School

A group of pupils are seen outside Moorpark School in the 1920s. At that time education was compulsory until the age of 14, the leaving age being raised to 15 in 1944. The Education (Scotland) Act of 1872 resulted in a national system of public elementary schools and made education compulsory for all children between the ages of 5 and 13. The local management of schools in Renfrew were under the control of Renfrew School Board from 1872 until 1918 when it was replaced by the County of Renfrew Education Authority. During the Second World War (1939-1945) over five hundred children were evacuated from Renfrew to outlying country districts because of the threat of enemy bombing. The following people were members of staff at Moorpark School in 1926: Louis N. Gow, M.A., B.Sc., Headmaster; Miss Isabella R. Stewart, Infants' Mistress; Henry Stuart, Continuation Class Superintendent; Miss Elisa B. Barbour, Teacher of Cookery; Miss Jean B. Craig, Teacher of Pianoforte; Angus McDonald, Janitor.

CONTROL TOWER FROM RUNWAY, RENFREW AIRPORT, SCOTLAND   D 563

6l. Control tower from runway, Renfrew Airport

A British European Airways plane and an Aer Lingus plane are seen on the runway at Renfrew Airport in this scene. It was in 1933 when several companies began internal air services from here. A service of flights began to Campbeltown, Islay and other islands. Allied Airways and Northern and Scottish Airways were formed in 1934. Scottish Airways was formed in 1937. This company also included Northern and Highland Airways. As a result of the Civil Aviation Act of 1946, British European Airways took over all air services. The number of passengers using Renfrew Airport in 1952 was 157,000. This figure had increased to 437,000 by 1957. By 1961, Renfrew was the busiest civil airport outside London. Freight traffic was also increasing rapidly at that time.

B.E.A. PIONAIR AIRCRAFT BEING SERVICED, RENFREW AIRPORT.

62. Renfrew Airport

A British European Airways Pionair aircraft is seen here at Renfrew Airport. This airport was originally laid out at Newmains Farm near Renfrew in 1916; it became Number 6 Aircraft Acceptance Park for the Royal Flying Corps and later for the Royal Air Force. In 1923 William Beardmore and Company founded a Royal Air Force Reserve Flying School at the airport. This was mostly for annual refresher courses. The school continued to operate until the end of 1928. Renfrew Airport also became the base of No. 602 (City of Glasgow) Squadron, Auxiliary Air Force from its inception in 1925 until 1933. From 1933 scheduled services began to operate from the airport. The airliner 'City of Glasgow' was at Renfrew Airport on 16th and 17th June 1928. Thousands of people came to the airport on these days to see the airliner or to take a short flight. Almost 2,000 people flew on the plane over the two days, the cost of a flight being just under fifty pence.

RECEPTION HALL, RENFREW AIRPORT, SCOTLAND

D 557

63. Reception hall, Renfrew Airport

Only a small group of passengers are seen in this view. Prior to the 1960s there was not the massive package holiday industry which exists today. Very little appears to be happening in this view, unlike a modern airport where there are crowds of people. From 1966 all flights left from the new airport at Abbotsinch two miles to the west of Renfrew. Abbotsinch was originally an R.A.F. Training Station which had operated there since 1932. It remained until 1943 and from that time it was operated by the Royal Naval Air Service. The Navy was still using the airfield in 1960. The necessity for the new Glasgow Airport was a consequence of the requirements of the jet age. It was not possible to increase the area of Renfrew Airport because of nearby obstructions and restrictions in further development.

MAIN ENTRANCE, RENFREW AIRPORT, SCOTLAND   D 5163

64. Main entrance, Renfrew Airport

There was rapid development of Renfrew Airport from 1946. It was formerly the Scottish headquarters of British European Airways. Similarly, the Scottish Air Ambulance service operated by British European Airways on behalf of the Department of Health for Scotland was based at the airport. By 1959 this service had carried about 4,700 patients and flown over 900,000 miles since its inception in 1933. A total of five hundred people were employed directly or indirectly at the airport by 1959. A maintenance workshop, which employed several hundred men, had been established by British European Airways in 1949, but this was transferred to London in 1955.

THE CROSS AND HAIRST STREET, RENFREW.

65. Cross and Hairst Street

A single-decker bus proceeds along Hairst Street in the 1950s. However, the tramlines and power lines are still in position. The properties on the immediate right beside the gable-end have been demolished. There is just one other car in the street and on the left some boys are admiring a stationary motorbike. One bus company, which had its origins in Renfrew, was that of Thomas Paton. He was a blacksmith who once had a cycle-repair shop in Fulbar Street. In 1921 he established his transport business with one bus. The Paton Bus Company had twenty-six vehicles by the late 1960s.

Cross & Bank Buildings Renfrew.

Published by Muir, Renfrew.

66. Cross and bank buildings

The people of Renfrew formerly travelled in the open-topped trams, which are visible in this pre-First World War scene. Very few people at that time possessed motor cars. The four ornate lamp-posts on the left were located outside the Town Hall. They are no longer in position. The four-storeyed building with the dunce's cap turret at Renfrew Cross belongs to the Bank of Scotland. New housing and shops were constructed to the right of the bank at 5-17 High Street in 1981-1983.

67. Monk Dyke

Monk Dyke in Alexandra Drive was formerly owned by Colonel Walter Brown of William Simons and Company, shipbuilders. He left this property in his will to the Burgh of Renfrew for such use as it might decide. Colonel Brown was the son of Andrew Brown, who was Provost of Renfrew in 1867-1870, 1879-1882 and 1891-1900. Monk Dyke was burned by incendiary bombs in the Clydeside air raids by the Luftwaffe in 1941. Until 1945 and for some time thereafter it had no roof. It was later restored and provided accommodation for the town council, the town clerk and his staff. There was also a council chamber, a provost's room, a lounge and a reception room. As a result of local government reorganization the councillors for Renfrew now meet in the council chamber in Paisley.

N. Gates, Robertson Park, Renfrew

68. North Gates, Robertson Park

Two well-dressed boys wearing caps stand at the North Gates of the Robertson Park in the early years of the twentieth century. A prominent notice-board near the entrance displays the various bye-laws concerning behaviour in the park. The police station with its distinctive architectural style can be seen in Inchinnan Road. There is a gap between the police station and the tenements on the right of this view. This site was later occupied by the Victory Baths which were built in 1921.

69. Argyle Stone and the Chariot of St. Conval

These two stones are situated about fifty yards from the east bank of the River Cart and about ten yards from Inchinnan Road. The stone on the right is the base or pediment of a Celtic cross, which was erected in memory of St. Conval, who was active as a Christian missionary in the surrounding area in the sixth century. Prior to the Scottish Reformation in 1560 many people visited this stone in order to seek healing from their various ailments. The stone on the right is now known as the Argyle Stone. Archibald Campbell, 9th Earl of Argyle, rested here in 1685 before being captured. He had refused to comply with the terms of the Test Act of 1681 whereby office-holders were required to adhere to the Protestant religion as defined in the Confession of Faith of 1560 and accept royal supremacy. He was condemned to death for treason but escaped to Holland. On his return he led a rebellion after the accession of King James Vll in 1685. On 30th June of that year the 9th Earl of Argyle was beheaded at the Mercat Cross in Edinburgh. The stone on the left is known as the Chariot of St. Conval and it is said that this was the stone which he first stepped upon when he landed here from Ireland. It is also where he said his prayers.

70. Town Hall

The Town Hall has been the subject of numerous photographs and post-cards because of its dominant position in Renfrew. In this view its size is emphasized when compared with the tram seen here in High Street. The flats and shops on the left at 6-24 High Street were built by the Renfrew Equitable Co-operative Society Ltd. These buildings continue as far as the kirkyard of the Old Parish Church. During the Second World War in June 1944 a mile of pennies for 'Salute the Soldier' week was laid in Renfrew. This began in the High Street opposite the Town Hall.

The Cross, Renfrew.

777/45

71. Renfrew Cross

An open-topped tram proceeds towards Paisley in this scene from the early decades of last century. It is bearing a prominent advertisement for 'Bovril'. A horse and cart can be discerned in Canal Street. The prominent lamp-posts on the left are no longer in position. Both properties on the extreme right of the turreted bank building have been demolished. This bank building, which is now occupied by the Bank of Scotland, was designed by George Washington Browne. By 1926 there were trams, which left Renfrew Cross for Glasgow every nine minutes. The last tram was at 11.21 p.m. Trams left Renfrew Cross for Paisley every twelve minutes till 12 noon and thereafter every six minutes until 10.48 p.m. The last tram from Renfrew Ferry left at 11.12 p.m.

Children's Playground, Robertson Park, Renfrew

72. Children's playground, Robertson Park

A large group of children gather round the maypole in this scene. Some of the boys are wearing caps in a style similar to those, which their fathers would have worn. Two of the girls are wearing boaters. On the left of this view a smaller group are seen at the swings. Tenemental properties are seen in this background and the police station is clearly visible in Inchinnan Road.

ROBERTSON PARK, RENFREW,   No. 1

73. Robertson Park

Some children pose for the camera beside the flagpole in Robertson Park. The houses in the distance are in Inchinnan Road. The spire of Renfrew Parish Church can be faintly discerned. This park continues to be a well-used facility. Mr. William Robertson, who was the original donor of the park, deserves due recognition for his foresight in providing this area for the people of Renfrew.

ROBERTSON PARK, RENFREW.

74. Robertson Park

A very young girl stands beside the swings on the right of this view and two more children are just visible on the left at the other set of swings. Climbing frames and a maypole can be seen. On each side of the large flagpole, two old cannons can be faintly discerned. The tenements in this scene are located in Paisley Road and Donaldson Drive.

At Renfrew ferry.

75. At Renfrew Ferry

An open-topped tram can be seen here in this view from former days. A steamer is also visible at the wharf on the right of the postcard. Between 1884 and 1903 many people from Renfrew sailed to Glasgow on steamers which were known as 'Cluthas'. There were twelve 'Cluthas' in total and they were numbered from 1 to 12. The 'Cluthas' carried from 230 to 250 passengers. Their peak year was in 1897 when a total of three million passengers were carried on these steamers. The fare for all sailings for many years was one old penny. However, as a result of the new electric trams at the beginning of the twentieth century and the subway in Glasgow, the 'Cluthas' ceased to operate.

76. Canal Street

A large group of children can be seen in this view from the 1890s. Some of the children are barefooted but all of them are wearing a variety of headgear. The business premises on the right are those of Leslie Kirk, painter and decorator, while on the left there is a tobacconist. The roof of this building is thatched in common with the neighbouring property. Part of a crow-stepped gable can be seen on the house on the left of this view beside the premises of the spirit merchant Robert Lang. All of the buildings seen here have been demolished.